Introduction

Salisbury Cathedral displays one of the only four original documents of Magna Carta surviving from 1215. To fully understand the origins and meaning of the Charter, we must first return to the years in which it was created.

On 15 June 1215, King John of England agreed to meet the extraordinary demands of his rebellious barons at

King John sealing Magna Carta in 1215.

Runnymede on the River Th[...] his seal to a document that has become known to us as Magna Carta, the 'Great Charter'. It is one of the most famous acts of any monarch in English history and one that reverberates around the world today in its significance.

For many, Magna Carta is the foundation of our modern liberties and human rights, ensuring equal treatment before the law. For others it represents the power of the people to restrain despots and their dictatorial rule. For others again it forms an early establishment of the principle of no taxation without representation.

Due process, the rule of law, consent to taxation … this is a lot to claim for a single sheepskin parchment which looks unremarkable to the modern eye: nearly eighty lines of closely written Latin text with no headings or subtitles or even a separate line for each of its sixty-three articles. But it is what it affirms that makes this document so special, with phrases and meanings that hold resonance to this day:

> – 'No free man shall be seized or imprisoned, or stripped of his rights or possessions … except by the lawful judgment of his peers or by the law of the land' (Clause 39).
> – 'To no one we will sell, to no one deny or delay right to justice' (Clause 40).
> – 'No scutage or aid [taxes] may be levied in our kingdom without its general consent' (Clause 12).

A monarch could no longer rule arbitrarily but only in accordance with 'the law of the land'. The impact of this precedent remains with us today.

Background

Four successive Kings of England: above, Henry II and Richard I; below, John and Henry III.

The events that led to Magna Carta in 1215 were dramatic and intense. The root cause of the trouble lay in the hands of King John, for it was his misrule that brought many of England's powerful barons together in a rare alliance that dared to challenge the authority of the king by force of arms.

Unsurprisingly, money lay at the origins of the discontent. John had come to the throne in 1199. Some historians believe that his brother King Richard the Lionheart bankrupted the country with his foreign wars and with the cost of the ransom to free him from prison when he was captured returning home from the Third Crusade. But other historians claim that this was not the case. All medieval kings had constantly to worry about financial issues, but it is the incompetent way in which John dealt with them that caused so much resentment.

Kings needed money primarily to wage their wars. John needed more money than most because as a knight and a general he was a failure; thus contemporaries mocked him with the nickname of 'Softsword'. In 1204 he lost large areas of land in France, including the vitally important Duchy of Normandy. He spent the rest of his reign trying to win these back and in finding the money to do so.

One method for collecting the money for his wars was a shield tax known as 'scutage'. This developed out of the feudal system and was designed so that barons and knights could avoid doing military service in the king's army by sending money instead, which John could then use to employ mercenaries (hired soldiers). John's father,

Henry II, levied eight scutages in thirty-four years; John levied as many as eleven in just sixteen. Furthermore, under John, the rate imposed reached a record high. Taxation and raising revenues for his wars increased across the land. Many barons and common folk felt that they were being exploited by the king. The 13th century Barnwell chronicler called John 'a pillager of his own people'.

Had John been winning his wars there would have been profits and benefits shared out; but the king kept losing. Major and hugely expensive campaigns in France failed to make any significant headway.

It is frequently claimed that Britain does not have a written constitution. This is incorrect. It does not have a *codified* constitution, in that its written components are not collected into one document. Magna Carta represents one part of the written constitution in its earliest form.

The disastrous battle of Bouvines in France in 1214.

John was not averse to blackmail. Official government records reveal that Robert de Vaux offered John 750 marks and five high-quality horses in order that the king 'would keep quiet about the wife of Henry Pinel'. Elsewhere they record that 'The wife of Hugh de Neville offers the king 200 chickens so that she may lie one night with her husband'. This may be some form of in-joke, but Hugh, a leading royal official, later deserted to the baronial cause.

King John hunting a stag with hounds.

In 1214 his most ambitious and costly military expedition yet was launched. At the battle of Bouvines, one of the most important battles of the Middle Ages, John's allies were defeated by the king of France. John's half-brother, William Longespée, Earl of Salisbury (whose tomb can be found in Salisbury Cathedral), was taken prisoner. In fact, John's allies had come close to winning the battle, for at one point the French king had been pulled from his horse and set upon, being saved only at the last moment by his bodyguard who sacrificed himself to allow his king to escape.

But the defeat was a decisive one. John, instead of recognising this, foolishly went ahead with yet another record-high scutage. This was too much for many barons. They were not prepared to see good money continuously wasted and the nation's wealth frittered away on military campaigns that were always failing.

Their grievances were compounded by other aspects of John's increasingly arbitrary rule. He also filled his coffers by corrupt manipulation of the justice system, a major concern expressed in Magna Carta. Other kings had manipulated justice, but none to the extent John did. Through the penalty system of amercements many people had to pay heavy cash fines for misdemeanours such as neglect of public duties. Thus Robert de Ros, Sheriff of Cumberland, was fined 300 marks for failing to keep some prisoners in custody. William of Cornborough died in gaol because he was unable to pay his fine. Many ordinary people were also charged regularly, often unfairly, with the minimum fine commonly amounting to over twenty per cent of a labourer's annual wage. (The concern is expressed in Clause 20 of Magna Carta.) Men were compelled to buy the goodwill of the king, even if they had done nothing wrong. Among the rebel barons were those who were in debt to the king and who were looking for a way to free themselves of this obligation.

John has been praised by some historians for being a good administrator who achieved high standards in proficient record-keeping in government. But this was actually a reflection of his failure and a cause of his downfall: he needed greater efficiency so as to exact more money to pay

Right: Justice is conventionally depicted as a blindfolded woman with a sword in one hand and scales in the other. This refers to the principle that the law is blind, treating all equally and fairly.

Left: Silver penny from the reign of King John, 1205–07.

Below: In King John's time, taxes were paid in commodities as well as money. (*Paying the Tax*, painted by Pieter Brueghel the Younger, *c*.1620)

Portrait of King John.

for his military defeats; and the way he ruthlessly pursued it drove more into the rebel barons' camp. A medieval king was required to be more than just a good book-keeper.

John was also a notorious womaniser, taking as mistresses and conquests the wives and daughters of some powerful men. Other kings had done this, but none so insensitively as John, and none in such a predatory way. His reputation in this regard was known even in France, where rumours spread that John had slept with the wife of his half-brother William Longespée when he was a prisoner of the French.

But there were darker and more serious stains against John's character. He was believed, almost certainly correctly, to have been responsible for the murder of his nephew, the sixteen-year-old Arthur of Brittany, a rival claimant to the throne of England.

A consequence of John's increasingly arbitrary actions was that even the greatest men of the realm felt their king could not be trusted and not even the most important of them were safe from his capricious actions. This personal fear added to their financial and judicial uncertainties and this led to direct action. The discontented barons and knights banded together under the leadership of Robert Fitzwalter the Lord of Dunmow, Roger Bigod the Earl of Norfolk, Geoffrey de Mandeville the Earl of Essex, Saer de Quincey the Earl of Winchester, Eustace de Vesci and other powerful lords, forging an alliance to curb the power of the king. Early in May 1215, they broke their homage to John and formed the 'Army of God and the Holy Church'. They had declared war on their king.

John suffered a number of losses, the most grievous of which was London on 17 May. With the capital and its wealth in rebel hands, and the barons now offering the Crown of England to Prince Louis of France, John was in serious trouble. The rebels drew up a document of their demands called 'the Articles of the Barons'; it was, in effect, the first draft of Magna Carta. The king needed to play for time. He therefore agreed to meet the rebels in mid-June at Runnymede. Magna Carta was about to become part of English law.

Right: The Articles of the Barons: the document in which the barons listed all of their demands on 15 June 1215.

Below: A king dictating the law.

Runnymede 1215

The Great Seal of King John shows him as a knight on one side and seated on the throne dispensing justice on the other. In reality, John failed at both.

By 10 June the king's men and advisers and the barons were at Runnymede on the River Thames, chosen because it was halfway between the barons' base in Staines and the king's castle at Windsor. Here the two sides pitched their camps and hammered out the last details of the impending agreement. One chronicler reports that 'nearly all the nobility of England' was there – an indication of how all understood the importance of what was unfolding.

The king's reluctant acquiescence to the Articles of the Barons was necessary to ensure peace. When he first heard their demands, one chronicler claims John had sarcastically snarled, 'Why do these barons not just ask for my kingdom?' But now he had little choice. The document, drawn up under the guidance of Stephen Langton, Archbishop of Canterbury, began with the words: 'These are the articles that the barons seek and the king concedes'. On 15 June John formally agreed to the terms and the king's seal was attached to the document. By 19 June final revisions had been made and Magna Carta became law.

This Charter of Liberties (as Magna Carta was called for the first two years) was largely preoccupied with financial matters relating to feudal payments and their regulation (Clauses 2–5, 6–8, 12–13, 15–16, 23, 28–31, 37, 43). Money and economic matters feature largely throughout: a number of clauses deal with debts, tariffs and scutage (Clauses 9–11, 26–27). The concern for justice was to the fore in clauses forbidding the sale of justice and the imprisonment of a freeman without trial by his peers (Clauses 39 and 40). The worry over the loss of patronage to foreigners, who were being appointed to leading positions, is also addressed.

The unsettled times are reflected in clauses calling for the release of hostages, the return of castles and the removal 'from the kingdom of all the foreign knights, crossbowmen, sergeants and mercenaries that have come to it, to its harm, with horses and arms'. The agreement was designed to maximise its broad appeal among the barons and to unite as many of them as possible against John's autocratic and capricious government.

King John had surrendered much of his power as monarch to his subjects. Such was his fury at this defeat that it is reported 'he gnashed his teeth, rolled his eyes, caught up sticks and straws and gnawed them like a madman, or tore them to shreds with his fingers'.

The most radical demand of all was the 'security clause', number 61. By this, the barons presented themselves as acting for 'the community of the realm' and, through a committee of twenty-five leading barons, they were to ensure, by force if necessary, that the king adhered to this agreement.

No one really expected the Charter to usher in a period of permanent peace. For the moment, it merely created a pause in the ongoing war between the king and his discontented barons.

Left: King John assents to the Magna Carta, 1215. Oil painting by Charles H. Sims held in the Parliamentary Art Collection.

Right: Statue of Stephen Langton.

The Magna Carta War

Below: One of the original 1215 Magna Cartas, owned by Lincoln Cathedral and currently on display in a purpose-built vault at Lincoln Castle.

Right: Rochester Castle.

By 19 June the first issue of what was to become known as Magna Carta had been written up by government clerks and copies sent to bishops and county sheriffs throughout the kingdom. This was the revised and, for the moment at least, final version that marked the solemn agreement between King John and his barons.

The Charter had done nothing to reduce the mutual mistrust of the opposing forces. Both sides delayed fully implementing their side of the bargain: John held on to his foreign advisers and men, and procrastinated on the return of lands and castles; the barons kept the Tower of London and some of them plundered royal lands. John appealed successfully to his ally and overlord, Pope Innocent III, who suspended Stephen Langton, excommunicated the rebels and annulled the Charter on 24 August. Both sides prepared for a return to all-out war. The Charter had lasted just ten weeks.

In September, John strengthened his network of royal castles and headed to his stronghold of Dover Castle to await mercenary reinforcements from the Continent. The rebels made for the strategically important Rochester Castle

which opened its gates to them. They needed such places because the king had a three-to-one advantage over them in castles. From here they appealed once more to Prince Louis in France. Louis made his military preparations to assist the barons while they waited for the king to begin his attack.

Below: A 13th-century fresco of Pope Innocent III in the Lower Church of Sacro Speco Monastery, Subiaco. Italy.

Right: The exiled Archbishop of Canterbury seeking refuge in Pontigny, from *Le Miroir Historial* **(translated by Jean de Vignay from Vincent de Beauvais's** *Speculum historial*), **1470s.**

The dramatic events of the two-year-long war that followed the sealing of Magna Carta are often forgotten. They involved a full-scale French invasion and occupation of England that was nearly a second Norman Conquest; the homage of up to two-thirds of the barons to the French prince as King Louis I of England; the death of King John; and the battle for the survival of Magna Carta.

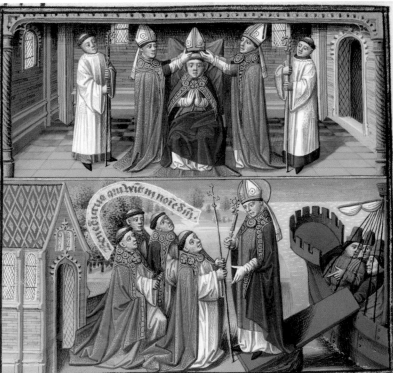

Some of Magna Carta's clauses seem particularly odd to the modern eye, such as number 33, demanding 'All fish-weirs shall be removed' from England's waterways. These weirs, however, inhibited movement and trade on England's rivers and thus affected people's wealth and livelihoods. Thus the Charter, for all its eclecticism, focused on and dealt with the real issues of its day.

Below: Effigy of William Longespée in Salisbury Cathedral.

Right: Prince Louis of France invading England in 1216.

John besieged Rochester with the might of his army in October. The rebels under their commander William d'Albini held out for nearly two months; they were so short of supplies they were forced to eat their costly warhorses. John's miners brought down a tower but still the garrison repulsed assaults on the castle. On 30 November they were finally starved into submission. John wanted to hang the entire garrison, but he was talked out of taking this drastic action.

John then took the war across the kingdom. Over the Christmas period of 1215 to 1216 he ravaged his enemies' lands from the south all the way to Berwick in Scotland in one of the most devastating campaigns the country has ever experienced. His mercenaries gained a notorious reputation for torturing and killing people for their money. The chronicler Ralph of Coggeshall reports that the king's troops 'made great slaughter everywhere they went'.

On 21 May 1216, Prince Louis of France landed on the Isle of Thanet in Kent with a large invasion force. John chose not to fight him and instead let the French forces land uncontested. Louis based himself in the rebel stronghold

of London. From there he set about conquering nearly half of the country, from Winchester up to Lincoln. Many royalists, seeing a genuine and positive alternative to John, deserted to Louis' side; among them was the king's half-brother, William Longespée, Earl of Salisbury. By the end of the summer, two-thirds of the baronage of England had expressed their support for Louis, recognising him as their new king. In September, King Alexander II of Scotland travelled all the way to Dover to pay homage to Louis as the new king of England.

The dichotomy between good and evil, and heaven and hell, pervaded the medieval mind and was often represented in art. King John came to symbolise all that was bad.

Below: An allegorical representation of Truth versus Falsehood from Salisbury Cathedral Chapter House.

Right: Sinners being led into Hell, in a detail of a medieval doom painting in the Church of St Thomas and St Edmund, Salisbury. Note that two of the sinners are wearing crowns.

In the south-east, only the great castles of Dover and Windsor held out against the French and the rebel barons. But just when the country seemed to be on the point of defeat, King John died at Newark Castle in October. Few tears were shed for him. One contemporary rhyme gave this damning verdict of his reign:

With John's foul deeds England's whole realm is stinking,
As Hell is, too, where he is now sinking.

Below: The coronation of Henry III.

Right: William Marshal unhorses Baldwin de Guisnes in a tournament.

Opposite: The siege of Lincoln: royalist forces under William Marshal defeat the French in May 1217.

John's death transformed the situation and saw a new emphasis placed on the Charter of Liberties sealed at Runnymede. His heir was his nine-year-old son, Henry III. Many of the barons who had resented his father could have no grievances against their new boy-king. With William Marshal, a leading figure of medieval chivalry and heralded as 'the greatest knight in the world', as regent, the royalists reissued Magna Carta at Bristol in November 1216 in an attempt to meet many of the demands of the rebellious barons and end the fighting. This first reissue dropped a third of the original clauses, especially the military-related ones and most notably 61, the security clause; it reflected that the country was in the middle of a major war of defence against a French invasion. The new, slimmed-down Charter did, nonetheless, promise to carry out the necessary legal requirements for good governance.

However, this still did not persuade enough barons to return to the royalist fold as Louis remained strong. William Marshal had to defeat the French in combat. He did this first at the battle of Lincoln on 20 May 1217. The royalist forces stormed into the city and killed the French commander there with a dagger plunged through the eye-slit of his helmet's visor and into his brain. Hundreds of prisoners were taken; many French soldiers were killed by townspeople on the roads as they attempted to make their way back to the safety of London.

Louis sent to France for help. A large army of reinforcements was gathered and set sail for England. On 24 August an English fleet went out to engage with it.

A bloody naval battle ensued off the coast near Sandwich in which the French admiral was beheaded and his fleet destroyed. It was one of the most important naval battles ever fought by England, for if the French had landed the war would have continued and Louis may well have succeeded in becoming king of England.

The French were forced to come to terms, and on 28 September Louis left England, never to return.

Magna Carta Triumphs

Magna Carta, the final version issued in 1225 by Henry III (vellum).

The war left England divided and politically and economically weakened. As part of the rebuilding process, the Charter of Liberties was issued for a third time in November 1217. Once again it was modified with deletions and additions, the forty-two clauses of the 1216 reissue now being increased to forty-seven. One of the major changes was the dropping of the four forest clauses (44, 47–48, 53). These were now incorporated into a new Charter of Forest Liberties. Thus from 1218, to differentiate between the two Charters, the larger Charter of Liberties became known as the Great Charter: Magna Carta.

From here it went from strength to strength in the 13th century. In 1225 it was reissued; as with the original of 1215, it was the result of a bargain being struck between the monarch and his subjects. Henry III needed money: in return for this reissue he received the proceeds of a general taxation.

Henry declared his commitment to Magna Carta nearly a dozen times during his reign, which lasted until 1272. By the 1250s the Charter was being copied out not only in Latin and French, but also in English, ensuring it became further embedded into the consciousness of the people. Each time Magna Carta was distributed among the shires and cathedrals of the land, it was sent out with the king's seal attached.

In times of unrest, crisis or financial need, appeals were made for the full implementation of the Great Charter. The 1225 Charter was reissued in 1265, again as the result of a second baronial rebellion: Simon de Montfort, wishing to see Magna Carta fully realised, had led the barons

Above: The death of Simon de Montfort, 4 August 1265.

Bottom: Historiated initial 'E'(dwardus) with King Edward I on his throne at the beginning of Magna Carta.

The 1225 Magna Carta is the definitive and enduring version that finally became enshrined in law. Pared down to thirty-seven clauses (some were dropped, others were merged), it begins by stating that these liberties were granted by the king 'of our own spontaneous freewill' and concludes with the promise that the Crown will do nothing 'whereby the liberties contained in this Charter shall be infringed or weakened'. Adherence to Magna Carta was thus established as the keystone of stable relations between monarch and subjects.

against the financial pressures imposed by Henry III to fund the king's failed foreign policy. In 1297, Edward I, needing, as ever, taxation to fund his wars, also reissued it. Under pressure from his subjects once more, in 1300 Edward announced what turned out to be the final reissue of Magna Carta. It had become a permanent feature of the constitutional landscape in medieval England.

The Salisbury Connection

Salisbury Cathedral holds one of only four surviving original Charters from 1215. Two are to be found in the British Library (although one of these is badly damaged by fire), and the last in Lincoln Castle. Although these are often called copies, there was possibly no single 'master' document of the Charter and all four are originals. At the time of distribution, all would have had King John's seal attached to them.

That Salisbury Cathedral holds one of the original charters is not surprising. Sheriffs of counties would deposit the Charter in cathedrals for safe-keeping. Salisbury's cathedral, an important institution in its own right, was in the capital city of Wiltshire. But there is a stronger connection: Elias of Dereham.

The difference between the surviving Magna Carta documents is striking, and indicates that they were written out by different scribes. It is estimated that around forty charters were produced, as each county probably received one. (Left: Salisbury Cathedral Magna Carta. Right: British Library Magna Carta.)

Elias is the canon who oversaw the planning and much of the construction of Salisbury Cathedral during the years 1220–45. He progressed quickly through the ecclesiastical ranks, moving from a secular clerk who became rector of Melton Mowbray and Harrow to canon of Salisbury Cathedral. He was closely associated with the great churchmen of his time: he was steward to Hubert Walter, justiciar of England and Archbishop of Canterbury (1193–1205), and his successor as archbishop, Stephen Langton (1207–28); and he also served another justiciar, Peter of Roches, Bishop of Winchester (1205-38). It was his closeness to Stephen Langton that makes Elias prominent in Salisbury's links to Magna Carta.

As mentioned earlier, Stephen Langton was central to the drafting of the Articles of the Barons and the Charter of Liberties. During the period 1208–13, Pope Innocent III wanted him to become the new Archbishop of Canterbury, but King John, suspecting Langton of being sympathetic to the French, refused. In the struggle that followed, England was placed under interdict and John was excommunicated: church services ended, and christenings and marriages were not recognised by the

All four Charters are written in Latin on a single piece of sheepskin parchment, but they display some minor differences. Their sizes range between 17 and 20 inches long (43–51cm) and between 13 and 17 inches wide (33–43cm). There are variations in colour, spelling and word order. The Salisbury Magna Carta is of special interest because it contains more errors than the others and is not written in exactly the same style (Chancery). In the rush to get the Charter out to all corners of the kingdom, different scribes were copying it and working under strict time pressures.

Church. In 1213 John had to submit to the Pope's wishes in order to gain his support against the barons. This involved handing England over to Rome as a fief and then receiving

Left: Statue of Elias of Dereham in Salisbury Cathedral.

Below: John, king of England, sends his submission to Pope Innocent III, 1213 (chromolitho).

it back as a vassal; John was supposed to pay the Pope 100,000 marks for it. Innocent III annulled the Charter in August 1215 because it violated his rights as feudal lord.

It was Elias who informed King John at Wallingford in May 1215 of the rebel barons' decision to break their homage to him and go to war. Elias was with Langton to negotiate the Charter and to witness the Runnymede agreement in 1215. His support for the rebels was made clear that year when he preached on their behalf in London. His importance was such that he was appointed as a commissioner charged with ensuring that ten parchments of the Charter were delivered safely, thereby bolstering the rebel cause.

When Innocent III, angry at Langton's role in the events, called the archbishop to Rome at the end of 1215 (and made him stay there until 1218), Elias joined the rebel barons' stronghold in London, becoming implacably opposed to the king and a dedicated supporter of Louis' attempts to become king of England. In his rejection of the cynical way in which King John and his government had sidestepped the Charter, the learned Elias provided the rebels with a strong intellectual foundation to their cause.

When negotiations for a peace settlement were first under way

between the English Crown and the French in mid-June 1217, Prince Louis rejected the terms because Elias and a few other close clerical supporters were excluded from the proposed treaty: Louis would only agree to the conditions if Elias and the others were compensated for the loss of their official roles. During the final negotiations in September, Louis was no longer strong enough to contest the same terms and so his loyal ecclesiastical ally Elias was punished with two years in exile. It is probable that his role in the Magna Carta war prevented him from reaching the highest offices in the Church.

On his return, as canon of Salisbury, he masterminded the plans for the new cathedral and oversaw the construction of the cathedral's east arm and the Lady Chapel, now the Trinity Chapel. He also had a house (Leadenhall) built for himself in the Close. This man of many talents died in 1245.

Salisbury Cathedral also has a connection to the 1225 Magna Carta. The Sheriff of Wiltshire deposited a copy in Lacock Abbey. This was the nunnery founded by Ela, Countess of Salisbury, wife of William Longespée, the first person to be buried in Salisbury Cathedral. Both she and her husband had been sheriffs of the county. This rare copy of the 1225 Charter is now in the British Library.

Left: Most representations of the sealing of Magna Carta give prominence to the Archbishop of Canterbury, indicating his and the clergy's key role in brokering the agreement. In this 19th-century bronze sculpture at Salisbury Cathedral, Archbishop Langton is shown advising the king.

Below: The medieval cupboard where Magna Carta was kept at Salisbury Cathedral.

Right: Salisbury Cathedral's east end, constructed by Elias de Dereham in the 1220s.

The Ongoing Legacy of Magna Carta

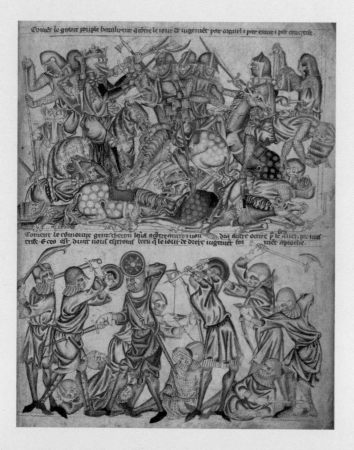

Peers and commoners fighting, 1320.

By the time of the last issue of Magna Carta in 1300, it was nearly a century old and in some ways feeling its age, many of its clauses seeming antiquated in light of a changing society. But in its fundamental affirmation of freedoms it remained deeply important.

The growth of Parliament, which was in no small part spurred on by Magna Carta, ensured its continuing relevance. For a long period in the Middle Ages, Parliament opened with a public reading of the Charter and made over forty renewals of its confirmation by the early 1400s. During the crises of weak kingship in the reigns of Edward II (1307–27) and Richard II (1377–99), both reflecting King John's own reign, the idea of baronial committees again came to the fore to play a major role in politics and the restriction of the monarch's power.

The reign of the powerful and effective King Edward III (1327–77) saw the further entrenchment of the Charter. In 1354 he extended its provisions beyond just freemen of the realm to encompass 'every man, of whatever estate or condition that he be'. Furthermore, he added that no one should suffer punishment without 'due process of the law'. In 1369 Parliament passed a statute that declared 'if any Statute be made to the contrary' of Magna Carta, it was to be ignored.

However, as the Middle Ages drew to a close, Magna Carta receded into the background. The upheaval of the Wars of the Roses (1455–85) was more concerned with the rivalry between competing kings than between monarchs and subjects. With the arrival of the Tudor dynasty (1485–1603) and the imposition of strong, royal government, especially under Henry VIII, and the further development of Parliament, there was little opportunity to extol the virtues of the Charter. Some Catholics tried to invoke its first clause protecting the independence of their Church against its absorption into the state at a time of Reformation, but to little avail. Many were wary of anything that might seem to promote rebellion against the monarch. Therefore, surprising as it may still be, Shakespeare's *The Life and Death of King John* (*c*.1595) makes no mention of Magna Carta whatsoever.

It was the great Crown versus Parliament crisis of the 17th century that saw Magna Carta propelled back to the very forefront of English constitutional politics. At this juncture it was the lawyers who called upon the Charter to defend the rights of individuals against what they saw as the growing despotism of King Charles I (r.1625–49). Once again, the Crown's need for money and the subsequent treatment of its subjects led to the dust being blown off the Charter. Charles attempted to bypass Parliament and impose a forced loan on the country in 1626; by the following

The Wonderful Story of Britain: King Henry and the Monasteries. Greedy courtiers' men carry away gold plate and jewels from a monastery. Painted by Peter Jackson in 1964.

summer he had imprisoned 150 men in London who refused to pay. When Charles re-established a number of feudal taxes that had long been forgotten and violated the Forest Charter, Magna Carta was once again on many lips.

Those who invoked the Charter presented it as part of Britain's ancient constitution and the birthright of her subjects and thus inviolable. As the lawyer Edward Coke declared, 'Magna Carta is such a fellow, that he will have no sovereign'. He reminded Charles that 'the king ought to be under no man, but under God and the law'. During the Civil War period of the 1640s the Charter was repeatedly raised as justification for resistance to an unjust and overbearing king.

As monarchy in Europe veered towards absolutism, Britons could feel that Magna Carta and the Bill of Rights afforded them some protection against such a direction. In 1762, when Arthur Beardmore was arrested for seditious libel,

Below: Attempted arrest of five members of the House of Commons by Charles I, 1642 (fresco 1856–66).

Right: Portrait of Edward Coke (1552–1634) from *Memoirs of the Court of Queen Elizabeth*, published in 1825 (w/c and gouache on paper).

he arranged things so that he was teaching his son Magna Carta at the time the officers of the law called at his house; this scene became a popular print that was circulated widely. When the French Revolution and subsequent Napoleonic Wars erupted (1789–1815), many in Britain then held up Magna Carta as a constitutional defence against political terror and dictatorship.

However, in the great reforming period of the Victorian age there was a comprehensive overhaul of legislation that repealed many old and outdated laws, including seventeen clauses of Magna Carta in 1863. By 1892 another five

Although the medieval meaning of Magna Carta was often misunderstood in the 17th century, it was the symbolism of what it represented that mattered most. Thus, when the English rebelled against King James II in 1688, Magna Carta was instrumental in shaping the consequent 1689 Bill of Rights. This 'Act Declaring the Rights and Liberties of the Subject and Settling the Succession of the Crown' forms the basis of Britain's modern constitution.

The 1689 Bill of Rights is read to the Prince and Princess of Orange by the Clerk of the Crown. Engraving by Samuel Wale, 18th century.

Left: Arthur Beardmore teaching his son Magna Carta © The Trustees of the British Museum.

Left: Magna Carta is so enshrined in American law that it is depicted on the bronze doors of the Supreme Court in Washington DC.

Below: Writing the Declaration of Independence in 1776. From left to right: Benjamin Franklin; John Adams; Thomas Jefferson.

were gone. Further revisions in the 20th century, such as the 1965 Law Commission's call for the removal of laws that were 'obsolete and superseded', meant that by 1970 only four clauses from 1215 (numbers 1, 13, 39 and 40) remained active in English law.

Yet Magna Carta still looms large in the public consciousness when it comes to ideals of political freedom and rights. One reason for this is that while the Charter declined in practical use in Britain, its importance had been growing across the Atlantic in the development of the United States of America.

English colonists establishing a new society in 17th century America deemed Magna Carta to be fundamental law, and thus took precedence over both Crown and Parliament. The General Assembly of Maryland in 1639 declared: 'The inhabitants of this Province shall have all their rights and liberties according to the Great Charter of England.' Before and during the American War of Independence, Magna Carta provided the colonists with an intellectual and constitutional rallying cry against what many deemed to be the tyranny of kings. The seal of the state of Massachusetts, designed by Paul Revere in 1775, depicts a militiaman with a sword in one hand and a copy of Magna Carta in the other. The 1791 Bill of Rights directly echoes Clause 39 of the 1215 Charter in its proclamation that no person shall be 'deprived of life, liberty, or property, without due process of law'.

Magna Carta holds great sway in the modern USA. Franklin D. Roosevelt declared in his inaugural address of 1941: 'The democratic aspiration is no mere recent phase in human history … it was written in Magna Carta.' It has been cited over one hundred times in the Supreme Court. To mark the legal and constitutional importance of Magna Carta, in 1957 the American Bar Association erected the memorial that now stands at Runnymede. The inscription carved into it reminds us why this ancient medieval parchment remains so relevant today:

TO COMMEMORATE MAGNA CARTA
SYMBOL OF FREEDOM UNDER LAW

It is this potent and enduring symbolism, celebrated worldwide on the 800th anniversary of Magna Carta in 2015, that will be celebrated for centuries to come.

Lord Denning, the most famous English judge of the 20th century, declared: 'Magna Carta is the greatest constitutional document of all times – the foundation of the freedom of the individual against the arbitrary authority of the despot.'

Left: The 3-shilling note issued by Paul Revere in the 1770s, a time when Magna Carta's importance as a symbol of liberty was at its peak.

Below: Mrs Eleanor Roosevelt addressing the 38th annual conference of the National Association for the Advancement of Colored People from the steps of the Lincoln Memorial in Washington DC, June 1947.

Magna Carta Translated

JOHN, by the grace of God King of England, Lord of Ireland, Duke of Normandy and Aquitaine, and Count of Anjou, to his archbishops, bishops, abbots, earls, barons, justices, foresters, sheriffs, stewards, servants, and to all his officials and loyal subjects, Greeting.

KNOW THAT BEFORE GOD, for the health of our soul and those of our ancestors and heirs, to the honour of God, the exaltation of the holy Church, and the better ordering of our kingdom, at the advice of our reverend fathers Stephen, archbishop of Canterbury, primate of all England, and cardinal of the holy Roman Church, Henry archbishop of Dublin, William bishop of London, Peter bishop of Winchester, Jocelin bishop of Bath and Glastonbury, Hugh bishop of Lincoln, Walter bishop of Worcester, William bishop of Coventry, Benedict bishop of Rochester, Master Pandulf subdeacon and member of the papal household, Brother Aymeric master of the knighthood of the Temple in England, William Marshal earl of Pembroke, William earl of Salisbury, William earl of Warren, William earl of Arundel, Alan de Galloway constable of Scotland, Warin Fitz Gerald, Peter Fitz Herbert, Hubert de Burgh seneschal of Poitou, Hugh de Neville, Matthew Fitz Herbert, Thomas Basset, Alan Basset, Philip Daubeny, Robert de Roppeley, John Marshal, John Fitz Hugh, and other loyal subjects:

1   FIRST, THAT WE HAVE GRANTED TO GOD, and by this present charter have confirmed for us and our heirs in perpetuity, that the English Church shall be free, and shall have its rights undiminished, and its liberties unimpaired. That we wish this so to be observed, appears from the fact that of our own free will, before the outbreak of the present dispute between us and our barons, we granted and confirmed by charter the freedom of the Church's elections – a right reckoned to be of the greatest necessity and importance to it – and caused this to be confirmed by Pope Innocent III. This freedom we shall observe ourselves, and desire to be observed in good faith by our heirs in perpetuity.

TO ALL FREE MEN OF OUR KINGDOM we have also granted, for us and our heirs for ever, all the liberties written out below, to have and to keep for them and their heirs of us and our heirs:

2   If any earl, baron, or other person that holds lands directly of the Crown, for military service, shall die, and at his death his heir shall be of full age and owe a 'relief', the heir shall have his inheritance on payment of the ancient scale of 'relief'. That is to say, the heir or heirs of an earl shall pay – 100 for the entire earl's barony, the heir or heirs of a knight 100s, at most for the entire knight's 'fee', and any man that owes less shall pay less, in accordance with the ancient usage of 'fees'.

3   But if the heir of such a person is under age and a ward, when he comes of age he shall have his inheritance without 'relief' or fine.

4   The guardian of the land of an heir who is under age shall take from it only reasonable revenues, customary dues, and feudal services. He shall do this without destruction or damage to men or property. If we have given the guardianship of the land to a sheriff, or to any person answerable to us for the revenues, and he commits destruction or damage, we will exact compensation from him, and the land shall be entrusted to two worthy and prudent men of the same 'fee', who shall be answerable to us for the revenues, or to the person to whom we have assigned them. If we have given or sold to anyone the guardianship of such land, and he causes destruction or damage, he shall lose the guardianship of it, and it shall be handed over to two worthy and prudent men of the same 'fee', who shall be similarly answerable to us.

5   For so long as a guardian has guardianship of such land, he shall maintain the houses, parks, fish preserves, ponds, mills, and everything else pertaining to it, from the revenues of the land itself. When the heir comes of age, he shall restore the whole land to him, stocked with plough teams and such implements of husbandry as the season demands and the revenues from the land can reasonably bear.

6   Heirs may be given in marriage, but not to someone of lower social standing. Before a marriage takes place, it shall be made known to the heir's next-of-kin.

7   At her husband's death, a widow may have her marriage portion and inheritance at once and without trouble. She shall pay nothing for her dower, marriage portion, or any inheritance that she and her husband held jointly on the day of his death. She may remain in her husband's house for forty days after his death, and within this period her dower shall be assigned to her.

8 No widow shall be compelled to marry, so long as she wishes to remain without a husband. But she must give security that she will not marry without royal consent, if she holds her lands of the Crown, or without the consent of whatever other lord she may hold them of.

9 Neither we nor our officials will seize any land or rent in payment of a debt, so long as the debtor has movable goods sufficient to discharge the debt. A debtor's sureties shall not be distrained upon so long as the debtor himself can discharge his debt. If, for lack of means, the debtor is unable to discharge his debt, his sureties shall be answerable for it. If they so desire, they may have the debtor's lands and rents until they have received satisfaction for the debt that they paid for him, unless the debtor can show that he has settled his obligations to them.

10 If anyone who has borrowed a sum of money from Jews dies before the debt has been repaid, his heir shall pay no interest on the debt for so long as he remains under age, irrespective of whom he holds his lands. If such a debt falls into the hands of the Crown, it will take nothing except the principal sum specified in the bond.

11 If a man dies owing money to Jews, his wife may have her dower and pay nothing towards the debt from it. If he leaves children that are under age, their needs may also be provided for on a scale appropriate to the size of his holding of lands. The debt is to be paid out of the residue, reserving the service due to his feudal lords. Debts owed to persons other than Jews are to be dealt with similarly.

12 No 'scutage' or 'aid' may be levied in our kingdom without its general consent, unless it is for the ransom of our person, to make our eldest son a knight, and (once) to marry our eldest daughter. For these purposes only a reasonable 'aid' may be levied. 'Aids' from the city of London are to be treated similarly.

13 The city of London shall enjoy all its ancient liberties and free customs, both by land and by water. We also will and grant that all other cities, boroughs, towns, and ports shall enjoy all their liberties and free customs.

14 To obtain the general consent of the realm for the assessment of an 'aid' – except in the three cases specified above – or a 'scutage', we will cause the archbishops, bishops, abbots, earls, and greater barons to be summoned individually by letter. To those who hold lands directly of us we will cause a general summons to be issued, through the sheriffs and other officials, to come together on a fixed day (of which at least forty days notice shall be given) and at a fixed place. In all letters of summons, the cause of the summons will be stated. When a summons has been issued, the business appointed for the day shall go forward in accordance with the resolution of those present, even if not all those who were summoned have appeared.

15 In future we will allow no one to levy an 'aid' from his free men, except to ransom his person, to make his eldest son a knight, and (once) to marry his eldest daughter. For these purposes only a reasonable 'aid' may be levied.

16 No man shall be forced to perform more service for a knight's 'fee', or other free holding of land, than is due from it.

17 Ordinary lawsuits shall not follow the royal court around, but shall be held in a fixed place.

18 Inquests of novel disseisin, mort d'ancestor, and darrein presentment shall be taken only in their proper county court. We ourselves, or in our absence abroad our chief justice, will send two justices to each county four times a year, and these justices, with four knights of the county elected by the county itself, shall hold the assizes in the county court, on the day and in the place where the court meets.

19 If any assizes cannot be taken on the day of the county court, as many knights and freeholders shall afterwards remain behind, of those who have attended the court, as will suffice for the administration of justice, having regard to the volume of business to be done.

20 For a trivial offence, a free man shall be fined only in proportion to the degree of his offence, and for a serious offence correspondingly, but not so heavily as to deprive him of his livelihood. In the same way, a merchant shall be spared his merchandise, and a husbandman the implements of his husbandry, if they fall upon the mercy of a royal court. None of these fines shall be imposed except by the assessment on oath of reputable men of the neighbourhood.

21 Earls and barons shall be fined only by their equals, and in proportion to the gravity of their offence.

22 A fine imposed upon the lay property of a clerk in holy orders shall be assessed upon the same principles, without reference to the value of his ecclesiastical benefice.

23 No town or person shall be forced to build bridges over rivers except those with an ancient obligation to do so.

24 No sheriff, constable, coroners, or other royal officials are to hold lawsuits that should be held by the royal justices.

25 Every county, hundred, wapentake, and tithing shall remain at its ancient rent, without increase, except the royal demesne manors.

26 If at the death of a man who holds a lay 'fee' of the Crown, a sheriff or royal official produces royal letters patent of summons for a debt due to the Crown, it shall be lawful for them to seize and list movable goods found in the lay 'fee' of the dead man to the value of the debt, as assessed by worthy men. Nothing shall be removed until the whole debt is paid, when the residue shall be given over to the executors to carry out the dead man's will. If no debt is due to the Crown, all the movable goods shall be regarded as the property of the dead man, except the reasonable shares of his wife and children.

27 If a free man dies intestate, his movable goods are to be distributed by his next-of-kin and friends, under the supervision of the Church. The rights of his debtors are to be preserved.

28 No constable or other royal official shall take corn or other movable goods from any man without immediate payment, unless the seller voluntarily offers postponement of this.

29 No constable may compel a knight to pay money for castle-guard if the knight is willing to undertake the guard in person, or with reasonable excuse to supply some other fit man to do it. A knight taken or sent on military service shall be excused from castle-guard for the period of this service.

30 No sheriff, royal official, or other person shall take horses or carts for transport from any free man, without his consent.

31 Neither we nor any royal official will take wood for our castle, or for any other purpose, without the consent of the owner.

32 We will not keep the lands of people convicted of felony in our hand for longer than a year and a day, after which they shall be returned to the lords of the 'fees' concerned.

33 All fish-weirs shall be removed from the Thames, the Medway, and throughout the whole of England, except on the sea coast.

34 The writ called precipe shall not in future be issued to anyone in respect of any holding of land, if a free man could thereby be deprived of the right of trial in his own lord's court.

35 There shall be standard measures of wine, ale, and corn (the London quarter), throughout the kingdom. There shall also be a standard width of dyed cloth, russett, and haberject, namely two ells within the selvedges. Weights are to be standardised similarly.

36 In future nothing shall be paid or accepted for the issue of a writ of inquisition of life or limbs. It shall be given gratis, and not refused.

37 If a man holds land of the Crown by 'fee-farm', 'socage', or 'burgage', and also holds land of someone else for knight's service, we will not have guardianship of his heir, nor of the land that belongs to the other person's 'fee', by virtue of the 'fee-farm', 'socage', or 'burgage', unless the 'fee-farm' owes knight's service. We will not have the guardianship of a man's heir, or of land that he holds of someone else, by reason of any small property that he may hold of the Crown for a service of knives, arrows, or the like.

38 In future no official shall place a man on trial upon his own unsupported statement, without producing credible witnesses to the truth of it.

39 No free man shall be seized or imprisoned, or stripped of his rights or possessions, or outlawed or exiled, or deprived of his standing in any other way, nor will we proceed with force against him, or send others to do so, except by the lawful judgment of his equals or by the law of the land.

40 To no one will we sell, to no one deny or delay right or justice.

41 All merchants may enter or leave England unharmed and without fear, and may stay or travel within it, by land or water, for purposes of trade, free from all illegal exactions, in accordance with ancient and lawful customs. This, however, does not apply in time of war to merchants from a country that is at war with us. Any such merchants found in our country at the outbreak of war shall be detained without injury to their persons or property, until we or our chief justice have discovered how our own merchants are being treated in the country at war with us. If our own merchants are safe they shall be safe too.

42 In future it shall be lawful for any man to leave and return to our kingdom unharmed and without fear, by land or water, preserving his allegiance to us, except in time of war, for some short period, for the common benefit of the realm. People that have been imprisoned or outlawed in accordance with the law of the land, people from a country that is at war with us, and merchants – who shall be dealt with as stated above – are excepted from this provision.

43 If a man holds lands of any 'escheat' such as the 'honour' of Wallingford, Nottingham, Boulogne, Lancaster, or of other 'escheats' in our hand that are baronies, at his death his heir shall give us only the 'relief' and service that he would have made to the baron, had the barony been in the baron's hand. We will hold the 'escheat' in the same manner as the baron held it.

44 People who live outside the forest need not in future appear before the royal justices of the forest in answer to general summonses, unless they are actually involved in proceedings or are sureties for someone who has been seized for a forest offence.

45 We will appoint as justices, constables, sheriffs, or other officials, only men that know the law of the realm and are minded to keep it well.

46 All barons who have founded abbeys, and have charters of English kings or ancient tenure as evidence of this, may have guardianship of them when there is no abbot, as is their due.

47 All forests that have been created in our reign shall at once be disafforested. River-banks that have been enclosed in our reign shall be treated similarly.

48 All evil customs relating to forests and warrens, foresters, warreners, sheriffs and their servants, or river-banks and their wardens, are at once to be investigated in every county by twelve sworn knights of the county, and within forty days of their enquiry the evil customs are to be abolished completely and irrevocably. But we, or our chief justice if we are not in England, are first to be informed.

49 We will at once return all hostages and charters delivered up to us by Englishmen as security for peace or for loyal service.

50 We will remove completely from their offices the kinsmen of Gerard de Athée, and in future they shall hold no offices in England. The people in question are Engelard de Cigogné, Peter, Guy, and Andrew de Chanceaux, Guy de Cigogné, Geoffrey de Martigny and his brothers, Philip Marc and his brothers, with Geoffrey his nephew, and all their followers.

51 As soon as peace is restored, we will remove from the kingdom all the foreign knights, bowmen, their attendants, and the mercenaries that have come to it, to its harm, with horses and arms.

52 To any man whom we have deprived or dispossessed of lands, castles, liberties, or rights, without the lawful judgment of his equals, we will at once restore these. In cases of dispute the matter shall be resolved by the judgment of the twenty-five barons referred to below in the clause for securing the peace (61). In cases, however, where a man was deprived or dispossessed of something without the lawful judgment of his equals by our father King Henry or our brother King Richard, and it remains in our hands or is held by others under our warranty, we shall have respite for the period commonly allowed to Crusaders, unless a lawsuit had been begun, or an enquiry had been made at our order, before we took the Cross

as a Crusader. On our return from the Crusade, or if we abandon it, we will at once render justice in full.

53 We shall have similar respite in rendering justice in connexion with forests that are to be disafforested, or to remain forests, when these were first afforested by our father Henry or our brother Richard; with the guardianship of lands in another person's 'fee', when we have hitherto had this by virtue of a 'fee' held of us for knight's service by a third party; and with abbeys founded in another person's 'fee', in which the lord of the 'fee' claims to own a right. On our return from the Crusade, or if we abandon it, we will at once do full justice to complaints about these matters.

54 No one shall be arrested or imprisoned on the appeal of a woman for the death of any person except her husband.

55 All fines that have been given to us unjustly and against the law of the land, and all fines that we have exacted unjustly, shall be entirely remitted or the matter decided by a majority judgment of the twenty-five barons referred to below in the clause for securing the peace (61) together with Stephen, archbishop of Canterbury, if he can be present, and such others as he wishes to bring with him. If the archbishop cannot be present, proceedings shall continue without him, provided that if any of the twenty-five barons has been involved in a similar suit himself, his judgment shall be set aside, and someone else chosen and sworn in his place, as a substitute for the single occasion, by the rest of the twenty-five.

56 If we have deprived or dispossessed any Welshmen of lands, liberties, or anything else in England or in Wales, without the lawful judgment of their equals, these are at once to be returned to them. A dispute on this point shall be determined in the Marches by the judgment of equals. English law shall apply to holdings of land in England, Welsh law to those in Wales, and the law of the Marches to those in the Marches. The Welsh shall treat us and ours in the same way.

57 In cases where a Welshman was deprived or dispossessed of anything, without the lawful judgment of his equals, by our father King Henry or our brother King Richard, and it remains in our hands or is held by others under our warranty, we shall have respite for the period commonly allowed to Crusaders, unless a lawsuit had been begun, or an enquiry had been made at our order, before we took the Cross as a Crusader. But on our return from the Crusade, or if we abandon it, we will at once do full justice according to the laws of Wales and the said regions.

58 We will at once return the son of Llywelyn, all Welsh hostages, and the charters delivered to us as security for the peace.

59 With regard to the return of the sisters and hostages of Alexander, king of Scotland, his liberties and his rights, we will treat him in the same way as our other barons of England, unless it appears from the charters that we hold from his father William, formerly king of Scotland, that he should be treated otherwise. This matter shall be resolved by the judgment of his equals in our court.

60 All these customs and liberties that we have granted shall be observed in our kingdom in so far as concerns our own relations with our subjects. Let all men of our kingdom, whether clergy or laymen, observe them similarly in their relations with their own men.

61 SINCE WE HAVE GRANTED ALL THESE THINGS for God, for the better ordering of our kingdom, and to allay the discord that has arisen between us and our barons, and since we desire that they shall be enjoyed in their entirety, with lasting strength, for ever, we give and grant to the barons the following security:

The barons shall elect twenty-five of their number to keep, and cause to be observed with all their might, the peace and liberties granted and confirmed to them by this charter.

If we, our chief justice, our officials, or any of our servants offend in any respect against any man, or transgress any of the articles of the peace or of this security, and the offence is made known to four of the said twenty-five barons, they shall come to us – or in our absence from the kingdom to the chief justice – to declare it and claim immediate redress. If we, or in our absence abroad the chief justice, make no redress within forty days, reckoning from the day on which the offence was declared to us or to him, the four barons shall refer the matter to the rest of the twenty-five barons, who may distrain upon and assail us in every way possible, with the support of the whole community of the land, by seizing our castles, lands, possessions, or anything else saving only our own person and those of the queen and our children, until they have secured such redress as they have determined upon. Having secured the redress, they may then resume their normal obedience to us.

Any man who so desires may take an oath to obey the commands of the twenty-five barons for the achievement of these ends, and to join with them in assailing us to the utmost of his power. We give public and free permission to take this oath to any man who so desires, and at no time will we prohibit any man from taking it. Indeed, we will compel any of our subjects who are unwilling to take it to swear it at our command.

If one of the twenty-five barons dies or leaves the country, or is prevented in any other way from discharging his duties, the rest of them shall choose another baron in his place, at their discretion, who shall be duly sworn in as they were.

In the event of disagreement among the twenty-five barons on any matter referred to them for decision, the verdict of the majority present shall have the same validity as a unanimous verdict of the whole twenty-five, whether these were all present or some of those summoned were unwilling or unable to appear.

The twenty-five barons shall swear to obey all the above articles faithfully, and shall cause them to be obeyed by others to the best of their power.

We will not seek to procure from anyone, either by our own efforts or those of a third party, anything by which any part of these concessions or liberties might be revoked or diminished. Should such a thing be procured, it shall be null and void and we will at no time make use of it, either ourselves or through a third party.

62 We have remitted and pardoned fully to all men any ill-will, hurt, or grudges that have arisen between us and our subjects, whether clergy or laymen, since the beginning of the dispute. We have in addition remitted fully, and for our own part have also pardoned, to all clergy and laymen any offences committed as a result of the said dispute between Easter in the sixteenth year of our reign [i.e. 1215] and the restoration of peace.

In addition we have caused letters patent to be made for the barons, bearing witness to this security and to the concessions set out above, over the seals of Stephen archbishop of Canterbury, Henry archbishop of Dublin, the other bishops named above, and Master Pandulf.

63 IT IS ACCORDINGLY OUR WISH AND COMMAND that the English Church shall be free, and that men in our kingdom shall have and keep all these liberties, rights, and concessions, well and peaceably in their fulness and entirety for them and their heirs, of us and our heirs, in all things and all places for ever.

Both we and the barons have sworn that all this shall be observed in good faith and without deceit. Witness the abovementioned people and many others.

Given by our hand in the meadow that is called Runnymede, between Windsor and Staines, on the fifteenth day of June in the seventeenth year of our reign [i.e. 1215: the new regnal year began on 28 May].